DATE DUE			
DEC 2 '97			
DEC 16 '98			
DEC 06 '99			
MAR 10 '04			
MAR 02 '06			

LUCRETIA MOTT

Early Leader of the Women's Liberation Movement

BY GERALD KURLAND

B. A. Long Island University
M. A. Brooklyn College
Ph. D. The City University of New York

D. Steve Rahmas, *A. B., J. D., Columbia U., Editor*

Compiled with the assistance of the Research Staff of SamHar Press.

SamHar Press
Charlotteville, N.Y. 12036
A Division of Story House Corp.

1972

Kurland, Gerald
Lucretia Mott, Early Leader of the Women's Liberation Movement. Charlotteville, N. Y.: Story House Corp. (Samhar Press), 1972.

32p. 22cm. (Outstanding Personalities, no. 39)
Bibliography: p. 32

1. Mott, Lucretia 1798-1880 2. Woman, Suffrage 3. Woman-Rights of Women 4. Suffrage 5. Emancipation of Women (Series: Outstanding Personalities)

HQ1410.M6.K8 923.96

(The above card has been cataloged by the editor and may not be identical to that of Library of Congress. Library card portrayed above is 80% of original size.)

Preassigned Library of Congress Catalog Card Number: 72-81902

LUCRETIA MOTT

Early Leader of the Women's Liberation Movement

When Lucretia Mott came of age in the early years of the nineteenth century, women had the same legal status as children and idiots: they were regarded as perpetual children, and from birth to marriage they were subject to the direct control of their father or other male guardians; after marriage they became the chattel of their husbands; in widowhood they reverted to being wards of their adult sons. From the birth of the republic to the Civil War, a woman could neither sue nor be sued, could not sign a legal document or draw up a last will and testament except with the express permission of her male guardian, and although she could own property she was not free to sell or otherwise dispose of it without male consent. Needless to say, women did not serve on juries, vote, hold public office, or have any legal voice in the determination of their future or that of their children. Every cent which a married woman earned became the property of her husband to do with as he pleased. If a woman broke the law her husband was held liable for damages. As late as 1850 it was even legal in every state of the Union for a man to beat his wife, provided the beating was not too severe. Indeed, Judge Buller of Massachusetts ruled that a husband could legally chastise his wife with a stick provided it was "no thicker than a man's thumb." Although a few exceptional women did succeed in becoming fully emancipated and in conducting their own affairs without male guidance, they were the exception rather than the rule. For the most part, nineteenth century American women were not judged competent to conduct their own economic affairs, and from cradle to grave they required male consent for everything they did. Lucretia Mott was one of those exceptional nineteenth century American women who rose above the legal restrictions and handicaps which plagued her contemporaries. She became one of the pioneers in the struggle to secure for women the same legal, economic, and political rights which men enjoyed.

NANTUCKET Located thirty miles off the coast of Cape Cod, Massachusetts, Nantucket Island was an important center of the American whaling industry, and Thomas Coffin (Lucretia's father) was one of those hardy men who pursued those magnificent ocean mammals. His family was of English origin, but unlike the Englishmen who founded the Massachusetts Bay Colony, the Coffins were members of the Society of Friends (commonly known as Quakers). Massachusetts' Puritan majority were not tolerant of religious minorities, and the Quakers were frequently the victims of religious and civil persecution. In order to escape the hatred of their neighbors, the Quakers began to settle on the remote island of Nantucket, which was only sparsely populated by the Puritans, and which soon had a sizeable Quaker population. The Coffins were among these Quaker families who established new homes on Nantucket, and in 1789 Thomas married Anna Folger (who was of the same family as Benjamin Franklin's mother). The couple had seven children, and Lucretia, their second, was born on January 3, 1793.

GROWING UP ON NANTUCKET At the end of the eighteenth century, Nantucket was still a primitive frontier community, and despite the legal distinctions which separated men from women, all frontier communities imposed a certain equality between the sexes. If their families were to survive and prosper, frontier women had to assume the economic and social responsibilities generally reserved to men in more settled communities. The Coffins were no exception to this rule. Thomas would often be at sea for six months at a time, and in his absence Anna would have to assume the burdens normally carried by her husband. In order to earn an income when Thomas was away at sea, Anna opened and ran her own grocery store. Besides putting in long hours of labor, Anna had to deal with wholesalers on the mainland, keep accounts, and prepare bills for her customers. Other Nantucket women performed similar economic functions, and Lucretia grew up in an environment in which men and women were social and economic equals and in which the legal inferiority of women was an irrelevant abstraction. After school, Lucretia helped her mother in the store and ran errands for her. Evenings her mother taught her the usual female arts of sewing, knitting, candle dipping, and homemaking. Lucretia was a typical American girl of the early nineteenth century. Brighter and more articulate than most girls, she was especially fond of talking, and her mother gave her the nickname of "Long Tongue."

BOSTON By 1804 Thomas had saved enough money to be able to give up whaling for a more sedentary trade, and by helping Anna with the grocery store during the off-season he had acquired valuable mercantile contacts. The couple decided to leave Nantucket and settle in Boston, which promised rapid economic advancement. That year Thomas entered into a partnership with Jesse Sumner and became a general goods merchant selling flour, candles, wines and spirits, sugar, oils, cotton, and linen among other items. The Coffin children were enrolled in the Boston public schools (Thomas declined to send his children to the more prestigious private schools on the grounds that they were "undemocratic"), and Lucretia became aware of the distinctions which society made between the sexes. Classes for boys functioned throughout the year, but girls were permitted to attend school only six months out of the year, and the Boston school system made no provision for the education of girls beyond grammar school (the present-day eighth grade). An inquisitive child who appreciated and valued education, Lucretia resented the restrictions placed upon the schooling of girls, and fortunately her father shared her feelings. Many nineteenth century families believed that girls should be educated only for careers as wives and mothers. Except for reading, writing, simple arithmetic, and the rudiments of moral philosophy, most Americans did not feel that girls needed or could profit from a formal, academic education. It was far better, they felt, to teach them how to sew, cook, and clean and care for a husband and children: a woman's proper place was in the home and she should be educated as a homemaker. Thomas, however, did not feel that way, and he was in a position where he could afford to give his daughters the finest education which society had to offer. His business was prosperous, and in 1806 he purchased a home in Round Lane for $5,600, which was then an enormous sum of money to pay for a house. When Lucretia completed her primary education at the age of thirteen, Thomas was determined to educate her further, and sent her to the Nine Partners Boarding School, a Quaker institution near Poughkeepsie, New York.

NINE PARTNERS James Mott (Lucretia's grandfather-in-law) was one of the nine men who founded the Nine Partners school, and he meant for it to embody the most progressive educational principles. The school did not disappoint his expectations. It was coeducational (although boys and girls attended separate classes), and combined Quaker religious training with the most up-to-date academic disciplines. Appealing to the reason and moral sense of its students, the school was among the first American institutions to dispense with corporal punishment. At Nine Partners, Lucretia studied modern poetry (her favorite subject), philosophy, economics, history, social theory and religious history. She quickly established herself as the school's outstanding scholar, and her academic performance was so brilliant that after two years at Nine Partners (while still only fifteen years old), she was offered an assistant teaching position by the school's trustees. In 1808 Lucretia became Deborah Rogers' assistant and taught reading, grammar, and arithmetic to the younger students. She also became aware of the social inequities which women suffered in nineteenth century society.

SECOND CLASS CITIZENS Deborah Rogers was a mature, experienced, and highly competent teacher; yet the salary which she received from Nine Partners was only one-quarter of the salary paid to young James Mott, Jr., who was hired as an instructor at the age of seventeen and had had no prior teaching experience. Even more unjust, Lucretia herself received no salary for teaching at Nine Partners, even though she did work that was equal to that performed by male teachers who were paid. It did not take her long to conclude that the economic discrimination suffered by women was based exclusively upon their sex and not upon any lack of talent or ability. She compared the disabilities faced by American women with the social equality that had existed between the sexes on Nantucket Island when she was growing up, and immediately sensed the social injustice that was being committed. However, Lucretia did not articulate her sense of outrage, and nearly four decades would pass before she acted on her conviction that men and women should enjoy an equal claim to the benefits of society.

PHILADELPHIA By the time she reached her seventeenth birthday in 1810, Lucretia Coffin had completed the course of study offered by the Nine Partners Boarding School, and since the colleges of that day did not accept women as students, her formal education was at an end. Accordingly, she went home to her family. The year before, Thomas had relocated his business on Dock Street in Philadelphia. Resenting the anti-Quaker prejudice which still ran deep in Puritan Boston, he decided to settle in a city where Quakers were accepted as equals. A few months after Lucretia had rejoined her family in their new Philadelphia home, James Mott, who had resigned his teaching position at Nine Partners, came to the "City of Brotherly Love" to pay a social call on the Coffins. He had developed a deep affection for Lucretia, and could not bring himself to stay on at Nine Partners without her. In the spring of 1811 they were engaged, and were married several months later; shortly thereafter James Mott became a partner in Thomas Coffin's business. Unfortunately, not long after their marriage, the United States went to war against Great Britain, and England's naval blockade of the American coastline threw the nation's business into a depression. Thomas Coffin's business suffered, and James was forced to take his bride to New York, where he found a job in a cotton mill owned by his uncle. As soon as the economic situation permitted, however, the Motts returned to Philadelphia, which became their home for the rest of their lives.

EXPANDING HORIZONS Between 1815 and 1827 Lucretia Mott suffered a series of family tragedies, and began to play an increasingly more important role in the affairs of the Philadelphia Quaker church. In 1815 she experienced a deep personal loss in the death of her father, but the birth of her first two children (a boy and a girl named for her parents) helped offset her grief. Seeking to ease the family's financial plight, Lucretia, early in 1817, took a teaching job at a Philadelphia Quaker girls' school. Later that same year, her son Thomas died and she was forced to give up her teaching job in 1818 because of her third pregnancy. Fortunately, James' business began to improve by the early 1820's, and he became one of the most prosperous commission merchants in the city of Philadelphia. Free now of financial worries, both James and Lucretia Mott began to take a more active part in the religious, civic, and charitable life of Philadelphia. Some time around 1818, Lucretia delivered her first public address at a meeting of the Women Friends for the Western District of Philadelphia. The Quakers were one of the very few religious denominations to accord women an equal standing with men in determining the affairs of the church, and they admitted women to their ministry. For Quaker women, their church was a vehicle for self-expression which enabled them to play an independent role in the life of their community. It was only natural that a woman of Lucretia Mott's ability would seek to rise above the deadening existence of a housewife, and it was equally natural that the Quaker church would be the arena for her development as a leader.

QUAKER MINISTER Quaker religious meetings are unstructured, and the minister rather than delivering a set sermon generally guides the discussion of the congregation which is free to follow its own inclinations. Since the deaths of her father and son, Lucretia had been a constant reader of the Bible, and when the spirit moved her that day in 1818 she rose to deliver a sermon which stressed the necessity of having unquestioned faith in God's omnipotence. Quite obviously, she was seeking to resolve her own religious doubts which came in the wake of her family tragedies, but her address was so moving and thoughtful that she was called upon to speak at other meetings of the Women Friends. Within three years, while only twenty-seven years of age, Lucretia Mott was ordained a full-fledged minister of the Society of Friends. Before long she would be involved in a series of trying sectarian squabbles. At about this same time, Lucretia read Mary Wollstonecraft's 1792 *Vindication of the Rights of Women*, which made a profound impression upon her and reinforced her determination to one day champion the rights of women. In addition, she accompanied Sarah Zane, a wealthy Quaker philanthropist, on a charitable trip to help the underprivileged people of northern Virginia. There she saw the operation of the slave system, and was reported to have been deeply affected by the plight of the Negroes in bondage.

OUTGOINGS The first occasion that Lucretia Mott had to express her own convictions came between 1822 and 1823; and it concerned the question of outgoings. Under Quaker religious discipline, members of the Society of Friends were not permitted to marry non-Quakers, and anyone who did so was considered to have left the church (hence, outgoing). Moreover, any Quaker who approved or connived at the marriage of a member of their family to a non-Quaker was also considered to have left the church. In 1822 Rebecca Paul, a widow and a member of Lucretia's congregation, was disowned by the Women Friends for approving the marriage of her daughter to a non-Quaker. Although Mrs. Paul appealed the decision, her expulsion was upheld, and Lucretia found herself in dissent from the opinion of the majority. She felt that that portion of the Quaker discipline which excommunicated members who married outside the faith was a denial of the very tenets which Quakerism embraced. In the first place it was a denial of the brotherhood of man and the essential equality of all men; and, secondly, it was a repudiation of Christian charity and forgiveness. While making her views known to members of her immediate family, Lucretia took no action to publicly express her feelings. She did not yet feel secure enough to defy the public opinion of her society; she had not yet emancipated herself from the restraints of her age; but she had taken the first step in that direction. In any case, in 1824 Lucretia suffered a double tragedy when two of her sisters died, and the grief she experienced prevented her taking a strong position on church matters.

ELIAS HICKS A native of Long Island, New York, Elias Hicks was responsible for a major schism in the ranks of the Society of Friends. He opposed the effort of the American Quaker community to emulate their English counterparts by drawing up a formalized Quaker dogma, and he doubted the validity of such orthodox religious doctrines as the Trinity, the divinity of Christ, the depravity of man, and the efficacy of vicarious atonement through the sacrifice of Christ. By 1827 his radical theological views had split the American Quaker community into a liberal (or Hicksite) faction and an orthodox (or anti-Hicksite) group. All Quakers, including Lucretia Mott, were forced to take a position on the religious issues raised by the Hicksites. She did not think it wise for the Quakers to adopt a formal dogma, because she believed that the spirit and moral qualities of religion were far more important than sectarian dogmas and institutions which often perverted the true spirit of religion. Unimpressed with doctrinal hairsplitting, Lucretia Mott believed that true religion consisted in showing one's love for one's fellowman, and that God was not in some far-off Heaven but resided within the human soul. In this respect she was very close to the Unitarians and the Transcendentalists, and she embraced the Hicksite doctrines. However, although she withdrew her daughter Anna from an orthodox Quaker school in 1827 and while her Hicksite sentiments were well-known, she refrained from publicly attacking the beliefs of the orthodox faction and managed to retain their respect and affection. Unlike many other Hicksites she was never disowned or condemned by the orthodox, and she continued to be re-elected every year as a delegate to the Yearling Meeting of the Philadelphia Quakers. Nevertheless, the schism was personally trying for her, and for the rest of her life she tried to avoid schismatic movements whenever possible. She had taken a stand, however, and was now ready to resist the tide of public opinion and champion unpopular causes.

ANTI-SLAVERY The first secular cause which Lucretia Mott embraced was abolitionism--a movement seeking the emancipation of America's Negro slaves--and ironically it was her experiences in the anti-slavery movement which pushed Lucretia Mott into a vigorous defense of the rights of women. The Quakers have the distinction of being the first organized American group to take a strong public stand against slavery, and their opposition to the institution of human bondage dated back to colonial days. The modern anti-slavery movement, however, dated only from the 1820's, and began when Quaker Benjamin Lundy (angered by the passage of the Missouri Compromise, which opened part of the Louisiana Territory to slavery) founded the *Genius of Universal Emancipation*, a newspaper which sought to appeal to the moral sense of Southern slave-holders and to persuade them to voluntarily free their slaves. Except for Quakers and New England intellectuals, the anti-slavery movement of the 1820's won few friends, and Lundy himself was frequently the victim of violence by Northern mobs which opposed the abolitionists. In 1831 William Lloyd Garrison, who had been an associate of Lundy, broke with his non-violent and gradual approach and organized the New England Anti-Slavery Society, which demanded the immediate abolition of slavery by whatever means were necessary. When England abolished slavery throughout its empire in 1833, the American anti-slavery movement was given a tremendous moral boost. If slavery could be abolished in the British Empire, why not in the United States of America? That year Garrison took the lead in organizing the American Anti-Slavery Society, and

James and Lucretia Mott were among the organizers of the society. Actually, Lucretia attended the organizing meeting only as an observer, not as a delegate, since women were not eligible for full membership in the Anti-Slavery Society.

THE PHILADELPHIA FEMALE ANTI-SLAVERY SOCIETY Back home James Mott was instrumental in forming the Pennsylvania Anti-Slavery Society, and for many years he served as president of the society. He was an important abolitionist leader and social reformer in his own right, but his services were completely overshadowed by the contributions made by his brilliant and talented wife, and he was generally known as Mr. Lucretia Mott. While James was organizing the Pennsylvania Anti-Slavery Society, Lucretia was busy forming the Philadelphia Female Anti-Slavery Society (she served as secretary of the organization), which concentrated its efforts on the improvement of the social, economic, and educational standard of the free Negro population of Philadelphia. The free Negroes of the North lived under severe restrictions. They could reside only in certain well-defined areas, generally could not vote or serve on juries, were not permitted to send their children to white public schools, and could obtain only the most menial employment. The Philadelphia Society maintained a school for the education of Negro children, and worked with Negro women to improve their economic skills and teach them how to be more efficient homemakers. It also relieved the economic distress of the most desperate Negro families, and generally operated much like a modern social welfare agency. Lucretia also began to preach at Negro church services, and, according to one observer, "Her noble countenance was radiant as the morning; her soft voice, though low, was so firm that she was heard to the farthest corner, and her little sermon /was/ as philosophical as it was devout...." As a result of her work among the Negroes of Philadelphia, Lucretia Mott earned a reputation as the city's outstanding reform leader. By the late 1830's the Mott home was a regular stopping point for intellectuals, reformers, and dignitaries visiting Philadelphia, and

Lucretia was becoming one of the best known women in the United States.

FREE PRODUCE In 1835 the Pennslyvania Anti-Slavery Society changed its policy to permit women to become full members of the organization, and Lucretia was promptly elected to membership on the society's executive committee, where she now had an opportunity to influence the development of the national policies of the American anti-slavery movement. She joined with her abolitionist colleagues to urge Congress to abolish slavery in the District of Columbia and in the Western Territories of the United States as a token of the nation's determination to right the evils of slavery. In addition, she also embraced the Quaker doctrine of Free Produce which would require all abolitionists to promise not to buy any commodity made through the labor of slaves. Hence, members of the society would refrain from wearing textiles made from slave-grown cotton, would give up smoking cigars whose tobacco had been picked by slaves, and would refuse to eat produce grown by slaves. However, in 1836, the American Anti-Slavery Society rejected the Free Produce doctrine on the grounds that it would adversely affect the business interests and economic livelihood of its members. It was one thing to advocate abolition; it was quite another thing to sacrifice one's economic interests for one's ideals! Indeed, the Motts faced this very question in the late 1820's, and answered it very differently. James had built up an extremely lucrative trade in Southern cotton, but when the slavery issue was brought forth as a moral and political question, he voluntarily ended his handling of cotton and developed an equally profitable trade in wool.

THE WOMAN ISSUE AND THE PHILADELPHIA RIOT In 1837 Lucretia Mott was instrumental in organizing the National Anti-Slavery Convention of American Women as an auxilliary of the American Anti-Slavery Society which still excluded women from equal membership with men. However, under the influence of Sarah and Angelina Grimke, the women's group adopted a strong platform demanding full equality for women within the Anti-Slavery Society. It was pointed out that there was an inherent contradiction between the abolitionist's professed desire to emancipate the slaves of America and their apparent unwillingness to emancipate the American woman from the shackles placed upon her by society. The Grimke sisters wanted to force the American Anti-Slavery Society to face up to the "woman question," and did not see how it could deny to women the fundamental rights it sought to secure for the slaves. While Lucretia supported the goals demanded by the Grimkes, she was not yet prepared to make an issue of women's rights. As a Quaker, she believed that reason and logic were still the most potent weapons in the world, and that once the men of the American Anti-Slavery Society realized the injustice they were committing then they would themselves remedy the wrong. Accordingly, she was content to let men like her husband James and William Lloyd Garrison present the position of American women and fight their battle for recognition for them. She was confident that their efforts would meet with success.

Meanwhile, the National Anti-Slavery Convention of American Women was preparing to hold its 1838 annual meeting in Philadelphia's Pennsylvania Hall, which had just been built by the abolitionists as a meeting hall and showcase to display the horrors of slavery. Unfortunately the lower classes of the white population, particularly immigrants and workingmen, were extremely hostile to the abolitionists. They feared that once slavery was ended, free Negroes would invade the Northern states, compete for their jobs, depress wage scales, and reduce their already too low standard of living. The abolitionists were considered by them as a threat to their economic well-being, and it was not uncommon for working-class mobs to break up abolitionist meetings and physically attack anti-slavery leaders. When the convention of American women convened, Pennsylvania Hall was invaded by a mob bent on destruction. At the entrance of the mob, panic swept the Hall, but Lucretia Mott quickly took the speaker's stand and pleaded for calm. She rallied the women to stand firm and resist the intrusion of the mob, and above all she urged them not to panic. The mob, however, would not be appeased, and the women had to be evacuated from the Hall for their own safety. Undaunted, Lucretia Mott invited the delegates to resume their meeting at her home on North Ninth Street. The victorious mob set fire to Pennsylvania Hall, and, their bloodlust still not satisfied, they set out for the Mott home to finish their deadly work. From her home, Lucretia and her guests could hear the shouts of the approaching mob, and could hear the ominous cry "on to the Motts." Fortunately, a quick-thinking male friend put himself at the head of the mob, and offered to point out the house to them. He led them on a wild goose chase and marched them far away from the Mott home. By the time the mob discovered they had been deceived, they were too tired and embarrassed to continue their hunt for the Motts. It was a harrowing experience, but as Lucretia later told friends, "I was willing to suffer whatever the cause required."

WOMAN'S PROPER PLACE William Lloyd Garrison and such liberal anti-slavery colleagues as Wendell Phillips were determined to squarely face up to the question of full membership for women in the American Anti-Slavery Society. At its 1839 meeting, they demanded that women be admitted to the society on an equal basis with men, that they be allowed to freely participate in debate and to hold national office in the society. The abolitionists, they felt, could not in good conscience condemn the South for holding slaves while they themselves kept their wives in a subordinate and slave-like position. However, the demand that women be given full membership in the society touched off a bitter and highly emotional debate which caused a split in the ranks of the American Anti-Slavery Society, and which weakened the movement as a whole. According to the social beliefs of the nineteenth century, women were morally superior to men, and were responsible for whatever moral, humanitarian, and social progress the human race had made. They exercised their power for good by instilling their moral virtues into their children and by moderating the savage and warlike spirits of their husbands, brothers, and sons. The reason that women were morally superior to men was because they were sheltered from the corruption and brutality of the world and confined to the wholesome environment of the home. The opponents of equal membership for women argued that if women were to take an active part in political and social controversies then they would become as corrupt and as hard as men. Once this occurred, they would be unable to properly raise their children, and the moral, humanitarian, and religious progress of society would be halted; society might regress and become even more brutal, corrupt, and evil than it already was. According to this view, woman's proper place was in the home and no good could come from taking her out of its wholesome influences.

VICTORY Lucretia Mott, attending the 1893 annual meeting as an observer, listened to the debates, and hoped that reason would triumph over narrow prejudice. As she did not believe that women were inherently inferior to men in intellectual capacity, so she did not believe that they possessed any claim to moral superiority. Although she could not actively participate in the debates, James Mott was an active champion of equal membership for women, and when the debates had concluded she had the pleasure of watching the American Anti-Slavery Society, by a vote of 180 to 140, agree to open its ranks to women on a basis of absolute equality with men. However, those who felt that equal rights for women must inevitably lead to the fall of Christian civilization left the American Anti-Slavery Society, and formed a men-only rival organization known as the American and Foreign Anti-Slavery Society. Others drifted off into the newly organized Liberty party which did not advocate the abolition of slavery as an immediate goal but simply sought to block its expansion into the Western Territories of the United States. In any case, with women now being accepted as members of the American Anti-Slavery Society, Lucretia Mott was elected to its executive committee for the year 1840. That same year, she was chosen as one of the representatives of the American

Anti-Slavery Society to an international conference of anti-slavery organizations being sponsored by the British and Foreign Anti-Slavery Society in London.
LONDON In the spring of 1840 James and Lucretia Mott, along with William Lloyd Garrison and the other members of the American delegation, set sail for England. It was to be a disappointing trip. After suffering badly from the effects of seasickness, Lucretia Mott arrived in London only to have the British managers of the conference refuse to honor her credentials! She was told that the recognition of women as delegates would lower the dignity of the assembly, and that she would be allowed to attend the conference, along with other women, only as an observer, and would have to sit in a special section reserved for her sex. Garrison, Wendell Phillips, and James Mott all protested that the managers were being unreasonable. They pointed out that as a recognized anti-slavery society they were invited to send representatives to the London conference, and that the invitation did not specify that the representatives had to be of any particular sex. Therefore, they maintained that the managers should concern themselves only with the legitimacy of Mrs. Mott's credentials, and that if they were found to be in order then she should be seated and treated like any other accredited delegate. Needless to say, the Americans were overruled, and to show his disgust with the British managers, William Lloyd Garrison sat with the women observers for the entire length of the proceedings.

Appealing the decision of the managers to the convention itself, James Mott filed a protest on behalf of the liberal representatives against what they considered to be the arbitrary and unwarranted decision of the managers. A floor debate was touched off which generally followed the same lines of the debate at the 1839 American Anti-Slavery Society convention. This time, though, there was a slight difference: the advocates of women's equality lost. It was later discovered that the people behind the decision to exclude Lucretia Mott from the conference were the orthodox Quakers who objected to her Hicksite beliefs, and that her sex was secondary to her religious beliefs as the basis for exclusion. Indeed, many English Quakers refused to receive the Motts during their stay in London. At any rate, Lucretia's treatment at the London convention seemed to have been the final incident which committed her to an active championship of women's rights. To be rejected by the British after fighting so long and hard for recognition by the American Anti-Slavery Society must have been a severe and humiliating disappointment. While attending the London conference, Lucretia Mott met Elizabeth Cady Stanton, whose husband was attending the meeting, and the two women were destined to work together in the struggle for equal rights for women.

THE CRISIS OF IDENTITY When Lucretia Mott returned home to Philadelphia, she was obviously disturbed and was trying to decide where her identity and allegiance lay. Should she continue to champion the cause of abolition, work to improve social conditions in Philadelphia, and accept the subordination of women; or should she instead boldly defy the conventions of society and strike out for the rights of women? It was not an easy decision for a genteel Quaker woman to make, and Lucretia did not decide to commit herself to the cause of women's rights without a good deal of soul-searching and personal anguish. While she was trying to make up her mind, she engaged in a host of activities. During the 1840's she helped to organize the Philadelphia Association for the Relief and Employment of Poor Women which sought to train poor women for productive employment in industry. At the same time she encouraged a movement which sought to redeem women from prostitution and help them find acceptance in society. In the decade from 1840 to 1850, Lucretia Mott traveled throughout the northeastern United States addressing abolitionist, religious, charitable, and women's organizations. Some of her excursions were not without unpleasant incidents. In 1842, while she was attending an anti-slavery gathering in Delaware, a slavery advocate removed the linchpin from her carriage, forcing her to remain in town while repairs were made. The local innkeepers, whose dislike of abolitionists was exceeded only by their dislike of Negroes, refused to serve her meals or to permit her to use their facilities. Despite these discouragements, she continued to actively champion the cause of abolition, and her extensive speaking tours made her one of the best known woman reformers in the country. When James retired from active business in the mid-1840's, he and Lucretia devoted all their energies to reform activities.

CHRONIC DYSPEPSIA During the 1840's Lucretia Mott became more forceful in the advocacy of her beliefs, and around 1844 she finally committed herself to women's rights. In 1842 she again found herself at odds with her church when she defended three Quakers, who had aided runaway slaves, from disownment by the church. Although the Quakers were opposed to slavery, as pacifists they did not approve of overt acts designed to injure slave owners or of violations of law on behalf of runaways. Lucretia condemned this attitude as an act of cowardice, and declared that abhorrence of violence did not mean that one had to stand idly by in the face of injustice and oppression. Practicing what she preached, Lucretia Mott allowed her home to be used as a way station for the Underground Railroad which helped runaway slaves escape to the safety of Canada, and when runaways were apprehended by the authorities the Motts took the initiative in raising the money to ransom their freedom from bondage. In 1844 Lucretia Mott lost her mother, and a short time later her only brother also died. The death of her mother helped bring on an attack of chronic dyspepsia, and for some weeks her life hung in the balance. During the course of her illness, Lucretia believed that she had received a message from her Inner Voice telling her to boldly speak her mind in public, and make a fight for the things she believed in, including the question of women's rights. After she had recovered her health, Lucretia remained true to her Inner Voice.

Publicly proclaiming her doubts about such orthodox Quaker tenets as the Trinity, the divinity of Christ, the depravity of man, and the vicarious atonement, Lucretia once more incurred the wrath of her Quaker friends. Nevertheless, she was held in such high esteem that despite her heretical views the Quakers never disowned or condemned her, even when she shocked their sensibilities by attending a congress of the Unitarian church when it convened in Philadelphia in 1846. No matter where she went, though, Lucretia Mott carried her message that American women were being grievously wronged by the inequitable laws of society, that women as well as slaves needed emancipation, and that they were entitled to the same civil rights as men enjoyed.

SENECA FALLS, NEW YORK "I grew up so thoroughly imbued with women's rights," Lucretia would later declare, "that it was the most important question of my life from a very early day." While this statement was somewhat exaggerated, the women's rights movement did become the major reform of her mature years, and she was, in fact, the most important leader of the early women's rights movement. In the summer of 1848, she finally had the chance to act on her convictions when she paid a visit to Elizabeth Cady Stanton at her home in Seneca Falls, New York. They had not met since 1840 when both had attended the London anti-slavery conference, and Mrs. Stanton, who had had one child after another, was unable to act on her ambition of forming an organization to work for women's rights. However, the Stanton children were now old enough to care for themselves, and over a cup of tea Mrs. Stanton and Mrs. Mott decided to launch the Women's Rights Movement. Prominent women leaders were invited to meet at Seneca Falls on July 18-19, 1848 to discuss the problems facing American women, and on July 14 notices were placed in the local press advertising the meeting. The only woman mentioned by name in the notice was Lucretia Mott, and Mrs. Stanton hoped that her fame would attract a large turnout of women and sympathetic males.

THE DECLARATION OF SENTIMENTS One hundred people (male and female) gathered at the Wesleyan Chapel in Seneca Falls to attend the first meeting of the Women's Rights organization. The most important leaders were Lucretia Mott, her sister Martha Wright,

Elizabeth Cady Stanton, Jane Hunt, Mary Ann McClintock, and the Negro abolitionist Frederick Douglass. Ironically, none of the women in attendance (including Lucretia Mott) felt adequate to the task of chairing the meeting and guiding its work, so that James Mott was asked to preside over the gathering as chairman. After discussing the legal disabilities under which women were forced to function, a Declaration of Sentiments, which followed the style of the Declaration of Independence, was drawn up. Remarkably modern and relevant in its language and expression of grievances, the Declaration accused men of conspiring to degrade, humiliate, and oppress women, and of forcing them to believe that they were inherently inferior to men. The Declaration demanded that the equality of all citizens before the law be extended to include women, and that they be granted all the rights and privileges which males enjoyed. More specifically, the Declaration demanded that women be accorded equal educational opportunity with men, especially on the college level and in medical and law schools. It asked that women be given equal treatment with men in industrial employment; that they receive equal pay for equal work; and that they be considered for advancement on the basis of merit and without regard to their sex. In addition, the rights of women to own property in their own name, to dispose of it as they pleased, to sue and be sued, enter into contracts, transact business, and act as guardians for their minor children were also demanded. Finally, and most controversial of all the demands made at Seneca Falls, was the demand that women be allowed to vote and hold public office. Lucretia Mott headed the minority faction which opposed asking for the right to vote, feeling that overt political activity was unladylike, and that women had no need for the elective franchise. However, Frederick Douglass' strong support on behalf of women's suffrage apparently tipped the balance in its favor, and it was adopted as one of the demands of the Women's Rights Movement.

THE STORM OF RIDICULE Lucretia Mott's name stood at the head of the list of the 100 people who signed the Declaration of Sentiments, and the Seneca Falls convention immediately bore a torrent of abuse from conservative newspaper editors. The New York *Herald* was one of the papers which castigated the "unseemly, unfeminine and indelicate exhibition" at Seneca Falls, and asserted that the women's demands were "old-maidenish, crochety, and idiosyncratic." It singled out Lucretia Mott (the apparent leader of the movement) for ridicule, and, comparing her to the Roman Lucretia, lamented that she "had not another Brutus to avenge the wrongs /being suffered/ from the horrible indignities and restrictions of male monsters...." The *Herald* concluded its attack by observing that "Lucretia the first raised a republic, Lucretia the second is bent on ruining one." If anything, the hostile reception accorded the Declaration of Sentiments only strengthened her determination to battle for the rights of women. Two weeks after the Seneca Falls convention, Mary H. Hallowell was elected first president of the Women's Rights Movement. Lucretia did not feel that a woman should actively lead the Women's Rights Movement, believing that a man could be much more effective in the effort to secure equal treatment for women. Nevertheless, she put aside her timidity when it was pointed out to her that men would not grant women equal rights unless women themselves showed that they wanted it and were willing to fight for it. Supporting Mary Hallowell, she declared that "Women should train themselves to take a dignified place in the world, to be rational companions, to share the responsibilities of life."

DISCOURSE ON WOMEN In December, 1849 Lucretia Mott became involved in her first public debate with a man, and delivered a defense of women which has become one of the classic documents of the early women's rights crusade. Richard Henry Dana, one of America's most respected lecturers and writers, addressed a meeting at the Philadelphia Assembly Building and declared that women could not have equal rights with men because they were inherently inferior to men in both physical and intellectual ability. He declared that both God and nature ordained women to be subordinate to men, and cited the Biblical injunctions commanding women to obey their husbands and women's lack of intellectual achievement to justify his position. Lucretia Mott was not in the habit of arguing with men as distinguished as Richard Henry Dana, but she did not feel that she could permit his arguments to go unanswered, and on December 17 she delivered her answer to Dana.

She answered St. Paul's injunction that women should be obedient to their husbands by pointing out that (1) St. Paul was a bachelor, who (2) advised men not to marry, and that (3) the moral and spiritual development of his age was not as advanced as that of the nineteenth century, so that the standards of his time were not necessarily applicable to the modern age. Moreover, with the past century, political rights, which had once been reserved only for the wealthy and noble-born, had been extended to all men regardless of wealth or birth. Slavery as well, which was once accepted as a natural part of life, was increasingly being condemned as the disgraceful remnant of a barbaric and unenlightened age. It was only natural to expect that the development of democracy and rational social thought would bring women into the mainstream of social, economic, and political life. Women, Lucretia Mott argued, could not long be denied the basic civil rights granted to all men as a matter of right. She then turned her attention to the supposed inferiority of women. Granting that the intellectual and social achievements of women were nowhere comparable to the achievements of men, she maintained that this situation existed not because women were inherently inferior but rather because men had repressed the intellectual development of women since the dawn of time. Denied equal education, forced to work for wages that were less than half of what men received, denied access to the professions and made to work at menial tasks, and denied all political and civil rights--with all these handicaps, it was to be expected that the intellectual achievements of women would be minimal and not equal to those of men. The cruelest aspect of this situation was that men cited women's lack of intellectual achievement to prove their inherent inferiority to men; and even more tragic was the fact that many women accepted this argument and actually believed themselves inferior to men and in need of their constant protection and supervision. According to Mrs. Mott, the lowly status of women stemmed not from biological inferiority, but from the systematic repression and oppression of men. Women had never been allowed to demonstrate their abilities and talents. Furthermore, even if it were true that women were intellectually inferior to men, "Does one man," she asked, "have fewer rights than another because his intellect is inferior?"

PRESIDENT OF THE WOMEN'S RIGHTS MOVEMENT

Over her vehement objections, Lucretia Mott was elected president of the Women's Rights Movement in 1852. Although she was reluctant to enter the public limelight, her colleagues felt that as the most distinguished woman in the country she was best suited for the task of presenting women's claims for equal rights. Between 1848 and the Civil War, the Women's Rights Movement had two principal objectives: the first was the passage of state laws recognizing the property rights of married women, and the second was the upgrading of the teaching profession. As president of the feminist group, Lucretia Mott led the fight for these objectives. and her labors met with a good measure of success. In 1848 New York State enacted a married woman's property law which recognized the right of women to own and control property independent of their husbands, acknowledged their right to the wages earned by their labor, and gave them equal rights of guardianship over minor children. The law was a milestone in the emancipation of women, and the feminists sought to have similar laws enacted in other states. The Women's Rights Movement acted as a lobby to pressure state legislatures into passing such legislation, and launched an educational campaign to persuade men of the justice of their demands. Mrs. Mott was deeply involved in this lobbying and educational crusade, and during the 1850's many states enacted their own versions of the New York State law, so that by the time of the Civil War women, while not first-class citizens, were no longer chattel and had some measure of control over

their own destinies.
EDUCATION Equally important to the Women's Rights Movement was the improvement of education, and with it the upgrading of the teaching profession. Women made up the bulk of the nation's primary school teachers by the mid-nineteenth century, and teaching was one of the few professions open to women. The reason for this, however, was that teachers' salaries were so low that only women would accept teaching positions, and even then women worked under special handicaps. Many school districts, as a condition of employment, required that female teachers remain single, and it was rare to see a woman teaching on the secondary school level or occupying an administrative position in the school system. In 1849 Lucretia Mott and her colleagues became active workers for Horace Mann's National Education Association, which sought to use political pressure to secure higher salaries for teachers, free them of unwarranted restrictions on their personal lives, and improve the quality of education which teachers received. At the same time, the Women's Rights Movement sought to increase women's access to higher education. Back in 1834 Oberlin College, which was a center of abolitionist sentiment, was the first American institution of higher learning to admit women as students, and in 1837 Mary Lyon founded the first women's college at Mt. Holyoke. The graduates of these institutions demonstrated that women could profit from higher education; many of them had gained entry to the professions, and some had become active workers for women's rights. Higher education was absolutely essential if women were to improve their position in society, and under prodding from Lucretia Mott and her organization more and more colleges (especially in the Western states) were opening their doors to women. In the 1850's, Elmira College became the first college to grant to women degrees equal to those given to men.

While president of the Women's Rights Movement, Lucretia Mott formally endorsed the Temperance Movement as a means of improving the lot of women by stabilizing family life. She shared the conviction that alcohol brutalized men, and that under its influence fathers neglected the welfare of their children, and husbands abused their wives. The effort to outlaw the manufacture and sale of intoxicating beverages through political action was supported primarily by women and Protestant clergymen, and was roundly condemned by urban males who identified women's rights with the crochety old ladies of the Temperance Movement, and they damned both groups. Lucretia Mott's identification with temperance probably hurt the women's rights cause. After addressing a temperance meeting in New York City in September, 1853, Lucretia Mott went on to address a meeting of her own Women's Rights Movement only to have the meeting broken up by hostile males who equated women's rights with the crusade against "Demon Rum." However, while crusading for women's rights Lucretia Mott did not neglect the anti-slavery movement which was now becoming a major political question.

THE SLAVERY AGITATION Between 1848 and 1860 slavery emerged as America's most vexing political issue. Briefly, the slave states demanded the right to establish slavery in the Western Territories of the United States, and insisted upon Northern enforcement of the Fugitive Slave Act, which required the apprehension and return of Negroes fleeing Southern bondage. The North, believing that slavery was both morally wrong and undesirable, was equally insistent that slavery be barred from the Western Territories and hoped to see the day when slavery, either by natural attrition or political action, would be eliminated from the social life of the South. On the issue of fugitive slaves, the Northern people were not willing to act as slave-catchers and return helpless and abused Negroes to the none too tender mercies of their masters. In the midst of this sectional hatred and turmoil, Mrs. Mott continued to play an active role in the fight against slavery. In 1852 she again advocated the Free Produce doctrine, only to have her colleagues reject it as likely to increase the number of Southern sympathizers in the Northern business community. A year later, Mrs. Mott courageously sallied forth into Kentucky, a slave state where abolitionists were far from popular, to address an anti-slavery gathering. Telling her audience not to condemn slave owners or impugn their moral worth, she urged her listeners to reason with them and try to peacefully convince them that slavery was morally wrong and that they should voluntarily free their slaves. Her conciliatory tone apparently disarmed the antagonism of a group of pro-slavery advocates who had come to disrupt the meeting, and she was not harmed. As a matter of fact, her reception in Kentucky was so cordial that she was led to believe that moral suasion could still be effective in bringing about abolition and that direct confrontation was unnecessary.

ADVANCING AGE By the mid-1850's advancing age and the effects of chronic dyspepsia forced Lucretia Mott to sharply curtail her activities. In 1857, wanting to take her away from the pressures and tensions of Philadelphia, James Mott purchased a home on the outskirts of the city on the York Road. Suburban life seemed to agree with her, and her health improved. Surrounded by her family of four daughters and a son, not to mention numerous nieces, nephews, and grandchildren, Lucretia continued to speak out on the issues of the day, even though she was no longer as active as she once had been. In 1859 she broke with the majority of her fellow abolitionists to condemn John Brown's raid on Harpers Ferry, Virginia. The demented Brown believed that God had commanded him to free the slaves by instigating a slave rebellion and arming them to murder their masters. His incipient rebellion was crushed by United States troops, and Brown was executed for treason and insurrection. To the Northern abolitionists, he was a martyr to the cause of freedom who had sacrificed his life in the struggle against slavery. Lucretia, however, saw the matter differently. Strongly opposed to violence, she did not believe that any good could result from armed attacks against the South, that such attacks were likely to make the South even more intransigent in its defense of slavery, and that John Brown was no better than an outlaw. However, her objections were not heeded as John Brown became a folk hero in the North and a symbol to the

South of the abolitionist desire to destroy Southern lives and property.

CIVIL WAR Within two years of John Brown's attack on Harpers Ferry, the South had seceded from the Union, fired on Fort Sumter, and started the American Civil War. Although she sympathized with the North and looked forward to the final abolition of slavery, she refrained from endorsing the Union war effort. Her Quaker principles would not let her support any war effort, and she was not convinced that there was any such thing as a just war. When the war finally ended, Lucretia Mott opposed the dissolution of the American Anti-Slavery Society, claiming that its work was not yet done. The mere abolition of slavery, she told her fellow abolitionists, did not mean that the Negro would automatically obtain the full rights of citizenship. She wanted the society to continue in operation in order to see that the American Negro obtained the education required by free citizens of a democratic society, and to lobby for congressional enactment of civil rights legislation on behalf of the Negro. However, feeling that the Freedmen's Bureau could adequately look after the former slaves, the American Anti-Slavery Society voted to disband. Nevertheless, those who agreed with Mrs. Mott that more remained to be done held an Equal Rights Convention in 1866. Her services to the American reform movement were recognized by naming her presiding officer of the convention, and it was agreed that an American Equal Rights Association would be organized which would work for women's rights as well as Negro rights. The Association actively supported the Radical wing of the Republican party and lobbied on behalf of the Civil Rights Act of 1866 and the Fourteenth Amendment to the Constitution which secured the citizenship rights of the freedmen. Unfortunately, the Equal Rights Association was as short-lived as the Radical Republican movement, and by the mid-1870's the nation had grown tired of reform, had abandoned the Negro to the white supremacists of the South, and looked upon women's rights as a joke. Mrs. Mott was now the grand old lady of American reform, and the nation's conservative mood did not discourage her. She was confident that idealism would one day return to America, and that the people would realize true equality for women, Negroes, and all oppressed groups. Until that day came, she was content to labor patiently and responsibly for her social goals.

THE LAST BATTLES In May, 1867 James and Lucretia Mott journeyed to Boston where they helped organize the Free Religious Association. Composed of Unitarians, Universalists, Transcendentalists, Congregationalists, radical Quakers, reform Jews, and non-sectarian radicals, the Free Religious Association was dedicated to the promotion of brotherhood among America's numerous religious groups and to a general uplift of the moral tone of society. Such distinguished figures as Ralph Waldo Emerson, Robert Dale Owen, and Rabbi Isaac M. Wise were prominent in the organization, and the only woman in the group was Lucretia Mott. At the same time, she served as vice-president of the Pennsylvania Peace Society, a predominantly Quaker society dedicated to the outlawing of war as an instrument of national policy. Unfortunately, in January, 1868 death claimed James Mott, and Lucretia never fully recovered from her loss. For nearly six decades James had been her constant support in the struggle against slavery and for women's rights, and his death deprived her of her main source of strength. However, between 1870 and 1875 Lucretia divided her time between Boston and her home outside Philadelphia. When in Boston, she regularly participated in the activities of the Free Religious Association as well as the Universal Peace Union and the Radical Club, which despite its ominous name was nothing more than an intellectual debating society whose members discussed the socio-economic problems of their day.

THE BATTLING SISTERS In the 1870's Lucretia Mott witnessed the splintering of the Women's Rights Movement into two hostile groups. The majority radical faction, the National Women's Suffrage Association, led by Elizabeth Cady Stanton and Susan B. Anthony, wanted to press for women's suffrage through direct political acitivity and wanted to liberalize the divorce laws so that women could more easily end bad and unwise marriages. The more conservative American Women Suffrage Association, headed by Lucy Stone, Mary Livermore, and Julia Ward Howe, strenuously opposed the liberalization of the divorce laws, seeing it as a threat to the stability of the family. In addition, they preferred to appeal to moral suasion rather than overt political activity in their campaign for the vote. Mrs. Mott did not believe in divorce and she had hoped that it would not have been made a "women's issue," but she also realized that any split in the Women's Rights Movement must inevitably weaken the movement as a whole and retard the realization of women's equality. Accordingly, she sought to use her position as the *grand dame* of the women's suffrage movement to bring the warring sisters together and bind up the wounds caused by the intramural squabbles. Unfortunately, her mediation efforts failed and the movement remained divided.

CLOSING SCENES In the mid-1870's death continued to strike members of Lucretia Mott's family and to take its toll of her will to live. In 1874 she lost her eldest daughter Anna, and only a few months later death claimed her closest and only surviving sister Martha. After 1875 the infirmities of age kept Mrs. Mott confined to her home and prevented her from being anything more than an observer of the life around her. On November 11, 1880 she succumbed to old age in her eighty-seventh year. She was eulogized as the most distinguished American woman of the nineteenth century.

Lucretia Mott lived to see slavery abolished in the United States. Though she did not live to see women achieve civil equality with men, she was instrumental in creating the movement which would eventually emancipate the American woman from the confines of the nursery and the kitchen. By her example, Lucretia Mott showed that women could play a meaningful role in the struggle for social justice, and that they were capable of achieving their own emancipation through their own efforts. Today, women still face a certain amount of economic discrimination in American society; but they have achieved a measure of personal freedom and legal equality which Lucretia Mott could not even have dreamed possible. It is doubtful that she would have approved the demands or the antics of the more radical members of the Women's Liberation movement, and she never considered men to be the implacable enemies of women. Lucretia Mott was one of the lonely pioneers in the cause of women's rights, and it is to efforts by her and her nineteenth century colleagues that today's women owe their civil emancipation and equality.

BIBLIOGRAPHY

BY LUCRETIA MOTT: Lucretia Mott's diary of her voyage to London and early anti-slavery activities has been edited by Frederick B. Tolles and published as *Slavery and "The Woman Question"* (1952). Her *Discourse on Women* (1850) is still worth reading. Anna Davis Hallowell's biography *James and Lucretia Mott* (1884) is of the "life and letters" variety, and contains the fullest collection of Lucretia Mott's letters and statements.

BIOGRAPHIES: There are three modern biographies: Lloyd C.M. Hare, *The Greatest American Woman: Lucretia Mott* (1937); Constance Burnett, *Lucretia Mott* (1951); and Otelia Cromwell, *Lucretia Mott* (1958).

SOCIAL HISTORIES: The social movements of the mid-nineteenth century and Lucretia Mott's contributions to American reform are covered in Alice Felt Tyler's *Freedom's Ferment* (1944); Edward D. Branch, *The Sentimental Years, 1836-1860* (1934); and, Fred L. Pattee, *The Feminine Fifties* (1940).

QUAKERISM: For Lucretia Mott's place in the history of the Quaker church, see Elbert Russell, *The History of Quakerism* (1942); and, Thomas E. Drake *Quakers and Slavery in America* (1950).

WOMEN'S RIGHTS: The best modern history of the women's rights struggle is William L. O'Neill, *Everyone Was Brave: A History of Feminism in America* (1971). Older but still useful are Elizabeth Cady Stanton, Susan B. Anthony, and M.J. Gage, *The History of Woman Suffrage*, (6 vols., 1881-1922); Belle Squire, *The Woman Movement in America* (1911); and Moisei I. Ostrogorskii, *The Rights of Woman* (1893). For collective biographies of the early feminists, see Gamaliel Bradford, *Portraits of American Women* (1919); and, Richardson L. Wright, *Forgotten Ladies* (1928). Useful in arriving at an appreciation of Lucretia Mott's place in history are biographies of her contemporaries and associates. Especially helpful is Alma Lutz, *Created Equal, A Biography of Elizabeth Cady Stanton, 1815-1902* (1940).